PETER LAFFERTY is a former secondary school science teacher. Since 1985 he has been a full-time author of science and technology books for children and family audiences, and has written over 50 books. He has edited and contributed to many scientific encyclopedias and dictionaries.

BETTY ROOT was the Director of the Reading and Language Information Centre at the University of Reading, England, for over twenty years. She has worked on numerous children's books, both fiction and non-fiction.

SHIRLEY WILLIS was born in Glasgow, Scotland. She has worked as an illustrator, designer, and editor, mainly on books for children.

BOOK EDITOR: KAREN BARKER SMITH
TECHNICAL CONSULTANT: PETER LAFFERTY
LANGUAGE CONSULTANT: BETTY ROOT

AN SBC BOOK, CONCEIVED, EDITED AND DESIGNED BY
THE SALARIYA BOOK COMPANY, 25, MARLBOROUGH PLACE,
BRIGHTON, EAST SUSSEX BN1 1UB, UNITED KINGDOM.
© THE SALARIYA BOOK COMPANY LTD MCMXCIX

PUBLISHED IN 1999 IN THE UNITED STATES BY FRANKLIN WATTS
AN IMPRINT OF SCHOLASTIC INC.
557 BROADWAY, NEW YORK, NY 10012
PUBLISHED SIMULTANEOUSLY IN CANADA.

ISBN 978 0 531 11825 2 (LIB. BDG.)
ISBN 978 0 531 15975 0 (PBK.)

VISIT FRANKLIN WATTS ON THE INTERNET AT:HTTP://PUBLISHING.GROLIER.COM

GROLIER PUBLISHING

A catalog record for this title is available from the Library of Congress.

PRINTED IN SHANGHAI, CHINA.
REPRINTED IN 2011.
18 19 20 R 12 11

WHIZ KIDS

CONTENTS

Wherever you see this sign, ask an adult to help you.

WHIZ KIDS
TELL ME HOW FAR IT IS

SHIRLEY WILLIS

W
FRANKLIN WATTS
A Division of Grolier Publishing
NEW YORK • LONDON • HONG KONG • SYDNEY
DANBURY, CONNECTICUT

WHAT IS DISTANCE?

The space between things is called distance.

Some distances are very small.

THERE IS NOT MUCH DISTANCE BETWEEN ME AND THAT SPIDER!

6

Some distances are very big. The moon is far away from the earth.

Distance can be any size.

7

WHICH WAY IS IT?

HOW HIGH UP CAN THIS LADDER REACH?

Distance can be measured in any direction — up or down, left or right.

HOW FAR DOWN SHOULD BORIS DIG?

The swimming pool is long in one direction and wide in the other.

WIDTH

LENGTH

I CAN SWIM ACROSS THE POOL BUT NOT TO THE OTHER END... IT'S TOO FAR!

9

CAN YOU GUESS DISTANCE?

You need to know the distance
from your home to your school
so that you can get there on time.

You can't measure every distance
— you have to guess
how far it is.

I'VE THROWN THAT BEAN BAG A BIT TOO FAR!

IS IT NEAR OR FAR?

You will need: Two bean bags

1. Place a bean bag at your feet as a marker. Throw the other one.
2. Measure the distance between the bean bags in steps.
3. Throw the bean bag again. This time guess if it has gone farther before you measure the distance in steps. Is your guess right?

Try guessing distances as you walk. Guess how many steps it will take to reach the next lamppost or the end of the road.

11

HOW FAR IS IT?

?

The distance between places is longer when a road is hilly or winding.

WHICH PIECE OF STRING IS LONGER?

Both pieces of string are the same length. One piece looks shorter because it twists and turns.
A road that twists and turns will be longer than a straight road.

IS IT THE SAME DISTANCE?

The distance between each house is the same. It doesn't take long to go from the first house to the second house: The road is straight and flat. It takes much longer to get to the third house because the road goes up and over the hill.

CAN YOU MEASURE DISTANCE?

Before there were rulers, people used their bodies to measure distance.

They measured short distances by thumb-widths or hand-spans.

Measure this page with your thumb. How many thumb-widths is it?

What else can you find to measure in thumb-widths or hand-spans?

HANDY MEASURES

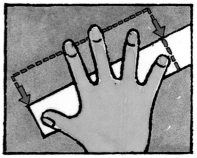

Stretch your hand out wide. The distance from your thumb to your smallest finger is called your hand-span.
(Mark your hand-span width on a strip of paper. You can use this to measure.)

Measure across pages 14 to 15 in hand-spans.

People measured
longer distances
by the length of their
foot, arm, or stride.

How many hand-spans tall are you?
Ask a friend to hold their hand on a wall to mark your height.
Now measure your height in hand-spans from the floor up.

THIS DISTANCE IS CALLED AN ARM-SPAN!

15

HOW DO WE MEASURE CORRECTLY?

GROWN-UPS' ARMS ARE MUCH LONGER THAN MINE!

Using the body to measure creates problems.
People are all different sizes, so their answers are different, too.

Hands are all different shapes and sizes — so are feet.

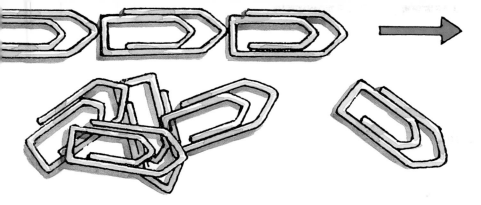

Measure this page in thumb-widths — is everyone's answer the same? Now measure it with paper clips laid end to end.
The measurement is the same every time because the paper clips don't change size.

If everyone used the same "lengths" to measure with, they'd get the same result.

STRAWS ARE GOOD FOR MEASURING, TOO!

17

WHAT IS A FOOT?

Although most countries of the world use the metric system, the United States uses a system of measurement based on inches, feet, and miles.

12 INCHES = 1 FOOT
5,280 FEET = 1 MILE

LET'S MEASURE

Put your thumb or small finger at the bottom of this ruler (right). Ask your classmates to do the same. Find out who has the biggest hand-span in your class. Who has the smallest?

A foot is divided into 12 equal parts. Each part is called an inch. 5,280 feet is called a mile.

INCHES

6

5

4

3

2

1

Put your thumb or small finger at the bottom of the ruler.

19

WHICH DISTANCE?

We measure
short distances
in inches (in).

IN IS SHORT
FOR INCHES!

We measure
longer distances
in feet (f).

F IS SHORT
FOR FOOT!

MI IS SHORT FOR MILE!

We measure very long distances in miles (mi).

MY SCHOOL IS 1 MILE AWAY BUT...

THE SUN IS 93 MILLION MILES AWAY

LET'S MEASURE

How big is this book — would you measure it in inches, feet, or miles?

How wide is it across pages 20 to 21?

How high is page 21?

Measure things around you. Try to choose the right kind of measurement each time.

WHY DO WE NEED TO MEASURE DISTANCE?

If shoes are too small, they hurt our feet.

HOW BIG ARE YOUR FEET?

You will need: A sheet of paper
Felt-tip pen
Ruler

1. Take off your shoes.
2. Put one foot on the paper and draw around it.
3. Now do the other foot.

Are both feet the same length? Measure them and see. Ask your friends to measure their feet too. Whose feet are biggest? Whose feet are smallest?

ONE FOOT MAY BE BIGGER THAN THE OTHER!

We measure things
for many reasons.

If a bridge isn't
long enough,
you can't cross
to the other side.

Furniture has to
be the right height
to be useful
and comfortable.

THE CHAIR IS
TOO LOW!

23

WHY DO WE MEASURE OURSELVES?

We measure ourselves so that clothes and shoes fit when we buy them.

We measure the height of babies and children to see if they are healthy and growing well.

THIS ISN'T MY SIZE!

24

MAKE A HEIGHT CHART

You will need:

A piece of wallpaper about 5 feet long
Felt-tip pen
Measuring tape
Thumbtacks
Stick-on labels

1. Pin the paper to the wall — this is your chart.
2. Get help to mark your height clearly on it.
3. Carefully measure and record your height beside the mark. (Measure from the floor up.)
4. Write your name and height on a label. Stick it to the chart beside your height mark.

Measure your classmates too.
Who is the tallest in your class?

You grow a little taller each year until you are about 20 years old.

CAN ROUND THINGS BE MEASURED?

The measurements of a round object have special names: the circumference, the diameter, and the radius.

CIRCUMFERENCE

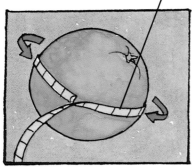

Measure all the way around an orange. This is the circumference.

DIAMETER

Take half an orange. Measure across the middle. This is the diameter.

RADIUS

Measure from the center to the edge. This is the radius.

The distance around
a round object is called
the circumference.

The distance across
a round object is called
the diameter.

THE DISTANCE AROUND
THE EARTH IS
24,900 MI

The distance from the
middle to the edge
of a round object
is called the radius.

27

How Far Away is the Moon?

The moon is 240,000 mi away from the earth.

Zoom!

This distance is so big that it takes a spacecraft 3 days and nights to reach the moon.

28

Imagine going around the world nine or ten times without stopping. That is like the distance to the moon.

A giraffe's neck can be more than 6 ft long.

Blue whales are the biggest animals on earth. They can be as long as 98 ft.

The tallest living thing in the world is a tree in California (366 ft).

The highest mountain in the world is Mount Everest (29,000 ft).

A flea is tiny, but it can jump 600 times its own body length.

THAT FLEA CAN JUMP A LONG WAY!

29

GLOSSARY

arm-span	The distance measured by the length of an arm.
circumference	The distance measured around a circle.
depth	The distance measured from the top down to the bottom.
diameter	The distance across the center of a circle. It is measured in a straight line from one side to the other.
distance	The amount of space between two points or objects.
foot (f)	A unit of length that measures 12 inches.
hand-span	The distance measured between the tips of the thumb and little finger when stretched apart.
height	The distance measured from the bottom up to the top.
inch (in)	A unit of length measuring one-twelfth of a foot.
length	The distance measured from one end to the other.
metric system	A system of measurement that is based on a meter length.
mile (mi)	A unit of length that measures 5,280 feet.
radius	The distance measured in a straight line from the center of a circle to the circumference.
thumb-width	The distance measured by the width of a thumb.
U.S. system	A system of measurement that is based on a foot length.
width	The distance measured from one side to the other.

INDEX